Jumping Into Revelation

-- The Midnight Hour --

A Prophetic Devotional

Jumping Into Revelation

Jumping Into Revelation

Copyright © 2018 by Overcoming Waters Publications

ISBN: 9781792118272

All rights reserved. This book or any portion thereof may not be reproduced or used in any manner whatsoever without the express written permission of the publisher except for the use of brief quotations in a book review.

Overcoming Waters Publications

OvercomingWatersPublications@gmail.com

Jumping Into Revelation: The Midnight Hour
Prophetic Devotional

Printed in the United States of America

First Printing, 2018

Facebook Fan Page
www.facebook.com/jumpingintorevelation
JumpingintoRevelation@gmail.com

Illustrations by Sara Hoover
TheSaraHoover.com
The.SaraHoover@gmail.com

"Scripture quotations are from The ESV® Bible (The Holy Bible, English Standard Version®), copyright © 2001 by Crossway, a publishing ministry of Good News Publishers. Used by permission. All rights reserved."

THE HOLY BIBLE, NEW INTERNATIONAL VERSION® NIV®
Copyright © 1973, 1978, 1984 by International Bible Society®
Used by permission. All rights reserved worldwide.

Scripture quotations marked (NLT) are taken from the Holy Bible, New Living Translation, copyright ©1996, 2004, 2015 by Tyndale House Foundation. Used by permission of Tyndale House Publishers, Inc., Carol Stream, Illinois 60188. All rights reserved.

Jumping Into Revelation

The world around you is dark and quiet...

the heavy chains press down on your weary arms, and your feet are held fast by a device that doesn't belong to you as the midnight hour draws nigh.

You endure prison smells, like rot and waste, for crimes you didn't commit. The sentence is too long and unjust. There is no mercy here and no comfort to penetrating aches. The darkness increases and your soul yearns for reprieve as the moon leaves the night to chase the sun.

Lift your head to the rafters! Behold the light is coming! Sing out with praise, for the Father of Lights comes at midnight, your darkest hour, to set you free! Rejoice and lead your comrades into shouts of triumph and praise to God for the hour of deliverance is here!

"About midnight Paul and Silas were praying and singing hymns to God, and the prisoners were listening to them, and suddenly there was a great earthquake, so that the foundations of the prison were shaken. And immediately all the doors were opened, and everyone's bonds were unfastened."

Acts 16:25-26 ESV

Jumping Into Revelation

Table of Contents

Introduction

1. **Do a New Thing** (Andrew Fulton)
2. **The Death of a King** (Allison Lozo)
3. **What's in a Whisper** (Andrew Fulton)
4. **Sweeping Words Caught in a Whisper** (Allison Lozo)
5. **Love** (Sarah Koch)
6. **A Father's Letter** (Aaron Longacre)
7. **Toy on the Top-Shelf** (Andrew Fulton, Aaron Longacre, & Aaron Loyet)
8. **A Walk in the Cool of the Day** (Andrew Fulton)
9. **Declarations: "I Am"** (Aaron Longacre)
10. **Farewell to Shame** (Sarah Koch)
11. **My Safe Haven** (Aaron Longacre)
12. **Theme-park Heaven** (Andrew Fulton)
13. **Deep Dive: John 3:8** (Aaron Longacre)
14. **Masquerade Party Invitation** (Allison Lozo, Andrew Fulton, Aaron Longacre, Mark Marini, Aaron Loyet, and Keene Fulton)
15. **A Brother's Plea** (Aaron Loyet)
16. **In Ageless Wonder** (Andrew Fulton)
17. **What is Real** (Sarah Koch)
18. **Cancer** (Aaron Loyet)
19. **Dear Self-doubt** (Andrew Fulton)
20. **A Cry from Atop** (Benjamin Mummau)
21. **A Warning Dream** (Andrew Fulton)
22. **The Chair** (Benjamin Mummau)
23. **The Sojourner** (Aaron Longacre)

24. **Prison Release** (Mark Marini)
25. **The Journey of Hope Part 1** (Allison Lozo)
26. **The Journey of Hope Part 2** (Allison Lozo)
27. **The Journey of Hope Part 3** (Allison Lozo)
28. **Trust** (Sarah Koch)
29. **Deep Dive: Colossians 2:15** (Aaron Longacre)
30. **The Love of the King** (Daniel Wagner)
31. **The Threshold** (Andrew Fulton)

Appendix:

Prophetic Dreams (Andrew Fulton)

Contributors to Jumping Into Revelation:

Aaron Longacre

Andrew Fulton

Allison Lozo

Aaron Loyet

Benjamin Mummau

Sarah Koch

Mark Marini

Daniel Wagner

Keene Fulton

Jumping Into Revelation

Introduction to Jumping in Revelation:
Prophetic Journaling Devotionals

You might be wondering what prophetic devotionals are and how they are different from any of the other devotionals available. It begins with the very source of inspiration, the Holy Spirit. After focusing and carefully listening to what He has to say, we simply write what He gives us, check what we received by the Bible, and came into agreement with His words.

Many people do this on a regular basis when they journal. These devotionals are much like that journaling, except that they are a collection of journal entries specifically given to each of us to place in this collection for you. We believe that the Holy Spirit has something special to say to you when you ask Him to use these devotionals to speak to you.

While in His presence, we listen closely to His words and watch for what He is showing us. We write down what we sense from Him. This comes by what we hear, see, smell, taste, and feel in our emotions or on our bodies. This might seem a little odd to some, but He truly has the ability to connect with us today as He connected with those we read about in His written word. More than that, He wants to! He suffered and died to make us His own (John 3:16-17). He is knocking on the door of our hearts and we are inviting Him in so that we can commune together in intimate fellowship (Rev. 3:20).

    He has the ability to connect with us in many more ways than we realize. This might sound strange to those that have become accustomed to sensing His presence in one or two ways, but He is much greater than our ability to perceive Him. When we open ourselves to Him, and become vulnerable, for the sake of increasing sensitivity and intimacy to Him, He connects with us in new ways that we had not previously known. He has connected with us by showing us pictures and visions, as well as dreams and visitations. He has also given us scents to smell and touches on our skin to communicate through discernment and provide direction to His will and purpose. We give Him the freedom to communicate as we sit at His feet like little children. When we write these experiences down they come in the form of poems, lyrics, stories, drawings, teachings, testimonies, revelations, illustrations, and declarations. You might begin to think that this is special, something set aside for certain revelatory people, but it's not. This is the New Covenant age! His presence and the ability to perceive Him is for everyone (Acts 2:17-18)!

The works compiled in this devotional include many of these revelations, not for the purpose of being the revelation, but to invite you into the revelation we have received. We believe that writing these revelations is an open invitation for you to cooperate with the Spirit where you are at the time you are reading this.

We invite you to find a quiet place in your morning or evening where you can be undisturbed. A place where you can feel the peace of the Spirit fall and rest on you easily. Then, as you carefully read each line, listen closely to the words, especially the words between the lines. There you will hear personal revelation from the Holy Spirit for yourself. He wants to speak to you and He has a lot of wonderful things to say. He is waiting for you, like a pool of fresh water on a hot day. Accept the invitation and jump into the revelation He has for you.

Each volume in this series will have a specific theme. The Midnight Hour is the chosen theme for this work, and for good reason. It is richly used in scripture to point out a special dichotomy. It is a time of transition that can go amazingly well or horribly wrong. The Midnight Hour is the time for repentance: followed by either deliverance or destruction for those that are determined not to change. Midnight is the darkest hour, but this is a good thing. It is the darkest of hours, but will soon fade away as the light of Jesus comes into your life to illuminate, guide, and bring life-giving energy into your darkened world.

Are you on the edge of night, a season of struggling against the flesh, loss of identity, confusion over direction, or weariness from spiritual warfare? The words written in this devotional are for you. May the personal words of the Lord reach your ears and find your heart as you read through this prophetic devotional. We pray that the journey through this devotional will lead you from the edge of night and into the glorious light of His presence.

Following each entry, there is space provided for you to journal, draw, or chronicle the words the Spirit gives you while you read. Be open. Be free. Be healed. Enjoy this special time, in Jesus' name!

Andrew Fulton

Jumping Into Revelation

Jumping Into Revelation

Do a New Thing

I've seen these walls before
None lead to an open door
Don't want to do this again
To the places I have been
My eyes look up to follow the floor
In search for something more

You said that You will do
Something good, something new
That the old has passed
This barrier will not last
Come and do, do what You do
Something new to get me through

I've wandered these halls before
Like following an endless floor
The corners all look the same
Progress is difficult to gain
A beginning looks like an end
Not losing ground is as a win

You said that You will do
Something good, something new
Lord, I wait for You
To move me through
Come and do, Jesus, what You do
Waiting for You, for You to move

"Behold, the former things have come to pass, and new things I now declare; before they spring forth I tell you of them."
Isaiah 42:9 ESV

Jumping Into Revelation

Ripples:

1.) Do you see God doing a new thing in your life?

2.) Are there old things keeping you from living in the new things He has for you?

3.) Do you believe God can bring something new out of tremendous loss?

Write what you feel, hear, or sense from the Holy Spirit

Illustrate any pictures or scenes

He shows you

Jumping Into Revelation

The Death of a King

"In the year that King Uzziah died, I saw the Lord sitting on a throne, high and lifted up, and the train of His robe filled the temple." Isaiah 6:1

There have been many great messages and teachings on the sixth chapter of Isaiah. This prophet was one who saw the Lord on a throne, his lips were cleansed, and he was sent by God. While there is a time and place to hear messages and teachings on the subject of being sent by God after we have an encounter with Him, there is another aspect of this passage that is often overlooked.

Please reread Isaiah 6:1 above. The part of the verse to focus on is "In the year that King Uzziah died..." A king is an authority figure. He is not merely a celebrity or a topic of hot news. In Isaiah's time, a king was a warrior, a protector, a provider, etc. And when a king died, there was grief over the whole nation, there was uncertainty if there were enemy nations around, and there would sometimes be chaos if a successor was not chosen beforehand. A father is an authority figure as well.

On November 30, 2017, my dad passed away unexpectedly. It was a devastating loss for my family. About a month later, there was a worship and prayer night at my church. The passage my pastor shared that night was Isaiah 6:1-8. As he read it aloud, I could not get past the first verse. I kept repeating it in my mind because I was living within the year that my father died.

There was grief, there was uncertainty, and there was chaos as I had lost my authority figure, my protector....... my dad. Even in the midst of all of that, there was a reminder that Isaiah had gone through a similar loss. And it was from this broken place that Isaiah saw the Lord in a way he had never seen before. That realization gave me so much encouragement in my brokenness that even in the midst of grief and uncertainty and chaos, there stands an opportunity for me to see God in a way I have never seen before; and this verse became a lifeline for me over the next several months.

If you are reading this today with the loss of a loved one, whether the loss is from this year or fifty years ago, there stands an opportunity in your grief to see God in a new way. He wants to meet with you. Let Him.

Ripples:

1.) **Has God brought something new for you out of tremendous loss?**

2.) **What revelation did you receive about authority, and how does it change the way that you view God and His love for us?**

3.) **What has the Lord whispered to you during this season of loss?**

Write what you feel, hear, or sense from the Holy Spirit

Illustrate any pictures or scenes

He shows you

What is in a Whisper

The strength of a father
The love of a mother
The request of a child
The tenderness of a spouse
The encouragement of a counselor
The secret of a sister
The schemes of a brother
The courage of a leader
The closeness of a friend
The call of the ill
The direction of a grandfather
The discernment of an uncle
The wisdom of an elder
The affirmation of an aunt
The care of a nurse
The fear of a sibling
The shyness of a new friend
The confidence of an old friend
The prayer of a grandmother
The song of a passing stranger

The voice of God

Listen for whispers today

1 Kings 19:11-12 (ESV)
"And he said, "Go out and stand on the mount before the Lord." And behold, the Lord passed by, and a great

and strong wind tore the mountains and broke in pieces
the rocks before the Lord,
but the Lord was not in the wind. And after the wind an earthquake,
but the Lord was not in the earthquake. And after the earthquake a fire,

but the Lord was not in the fire. And after the fire
The sound of a low whisper." (Emphasis added)

Ripples:

1.) What is the Lord whispering to you?

2.) Have you recognized when the Lord has whispered to you through others, like an example above?

3.) Listen closely today for the Spirit's whisper of encouragement, direction, and preparation for your next season.

Write what you feel, hear, or sense from the Holy Spirit

Illustrate any pictures or scenes

He shows you

Jumping Into Revelation

"Sweeping Words Caught in a Whisper"

There is a shadow that soon will pass.
There is despair that will fade like grass.
My child will soon blossom and come into the light,
But first you must pass through the darkest of night.

I am always with you, this you have known,
And I am very proud of the way you have grown.
You are facing the world with its rights and its wrongs,
And you will remember that I AM never gone.

The promises I made to you will come to pass,
But first you must willingly go through your past;
All the judgments and abuse, all the pain and the fears,
I'll be there the whole way drying your tears.

Before you can go on you must first go back
To the very first time; even before the attack.
Your future is bright; you know this very well,
Even though it feels like you just went through hell.

You look to the future, so bright and so new,
And say to yourself, "What now do I do?"
I will be with you, to lead and to guide,
There is nothing to fear when I'm here by your side.

There's something about you that makes Me smile
And that is because you are My child.
Even when you walk through the darkest of night,
My Word is in you, you are the light!

Wherever you walk, wherever you tread,
Don't think of the task, think of Me instead.
I have given you gifts to be used for My glory.
You are a small piece in a much bigger story.

But don't you dare think you're insignificant and small,
For even the biggest puzzles need pieces one and all.
The gifts I have given you were given for a reason,
Even though they may stay for only a season.

With each new day, My promises are renewed,
And the power of My love makes you new too.
So go out and say how your life is changed,
And I promise you this, you'll never be the same.

Ripples:

1.) What did the Lord say when you listened for His whispers of encouragement, direction, and preparation?

2.) When has the Lord taken you through your "darkest of night"? Are you currently in your "darkness of night"?

3.) Are you willing to let the love of the Father reach you in your darkest pain?

Write what you feel, hear, or sense from the Holy Spirit

Illustrate any pictures or scenes

He shows you

Jumping Into Revelation

Love

Love is sacrifice.
Love is choice.
Love is beauty.
Love has a voice –
Do you hear it?

Love is danger.
Love is grace.
Love is freedom.
Love has a face –
Do you see it?

Love continues.
Love goes on.
Love forgives.
Love moves on.
Do you choose it?

Love cannot hide.
Love cannot lie.
Love cannot hate.
Love cannot die.
Do you believe it?

Love is enduring.
Love is kind.
Love is patient

Love does not blind.
Will you search for it?

Love's not a compromise.
It is no illusion.
Love is reality.
Love knows no confusion.

Love has no beginning.
It has no end.
Love does not change.
It does not bend.

Love is eternity.
Love is life.
Love is hope.
Love grows in strife.

Love is a rose.
It is a gift.
Love is priceless.
It does not shift.

Love is selfless.
Love is just.
Love is humble.
Love is trust.

Love is simple.

It is like a child.
Love is untamable.
Love is wild.

Love is unchangeable.
Love is unfadable.
Love is undefeatable.
Love is unforgettable.
Love... is.

Love is dancing.
Love is singing.
Love is writing.
Love is bringing
what you have
to the One
who has it all.

Love is simple.
Love is beautiful.
Love is childlike.
Love is truthful.
Love is trusting.
Love is enduring.
Love is faith.
Love is hope.
Love... is.

1 John 4:8 (NIV): "Whoever does not love does not know God, because God is love."

1 Corinthians 13:4-8 (NIV): "Love is patient, love is kind. It does not envy, it does not boast, it is not proud. It does not dishonor others, it is not self-seeking, it is not easily angered, it keeps no record of wrongs. Love does not delight in evil but rejoices with the truth. It always protects, always trusts, always hopes, always perseveres. Love never fails. But where there are prophecies, they will cease; where there are tongues, they will be stilled; where there is knowledge, it will pass away."

1 Corinthians 13:13 (NIV): "And now these three remain: faith, hope and love. But the greatest of these is love."

Song of Solomon 8:6-7 (NIV): "Hold me close to your heart like the seal around your neck. Keep me close to yourself like the ring on your finger. My love for you is so strong it won't let you go. Love is as powerful as death. Love's jealousy is as strong as the grave. Love is like a blazing fire. It burns like a mighty flame. No amount of water can put it out. Rivers can't drown it. Suppose someone offers all of his wealth to buy love. That won't even come close to being enough."

Ripples:

1.) How have you experienced the love of the Father?

2.) Have you ever received a hug from Abba? Did you know that He loves to hug His children?

> *Find a safe quiet place and focus on the Father's love. Picture Him scooping you into His arms with a steady warm embrace. Don't be surprised if you feel His warmth across your chest.*

3.) Are you ready to rest in His love for you during times of pruning and preparation ahead?

Write what you feel, hear, or sense from the Holy Spirit

Illustrate any pictures or scenes

He shows you

Jumping Into Revelation

A Father's Letter

My beloved child,

    I'm writing this letter to share My heart with you. I've watched over you these many years and have seen you grow, and live, and learn through it all. First and foremost, I want you to know that I'm so proud of you. You've been through many hardships and personal struggles, and I know that it hasn't been easy for you. Life isn't always easy, nor did I ever tell you that it would be...and even though you've had so many questions and so many heartaches you've always turned to Me for guidance. That makes My heart glad. It always brings Me joy to see you look to Me in trust. Just know that I see it all.
    I haven't turned away from you. I haven't ignored you. And yes, I do care about how much it hurt. I put you in this particular place to grow and to be consistently dependent upon Me. I know that you want to be strong by yourself, but I know that that isn't enough. Besides, you

don't need to do this alone; Your Father is always with you.

    You tried so hard for so long to prove to Me that you were worthy...but you don't understand, I never asked for that. You're already worthy because you're My child and I made you expressly for My love. There isn't a thing you could do to make Me love you any more, nor is there a single thing that can separate you from My persistent love. Just trust Me to guide you and uphold you through it all.

    I want to give you My strength. Will you receive it? I want to instill you with My wisdom. Will you accept it? I want to shower you with My grace. Will you cherish it? All that I am, I give to you. That is My legacy that I entrust to you. My most precious treasure freely given to My most precious person.

    When you step out into this cruel and unloving world, remember that you carry My heart of compassion wherever you go. When the weight becomes too great, just listen for My voice within and I'll comfort you. I love you very much!

Always and forever,

```
Your loving Father
```

Ripples:

1.) Are you ready to rest in His love for you during times of pruning and preparation ahead?

2.) During times of trial and difficulty, have you allowed the Lord to better you, or have you allowed yourself to become bitter?

3.) Have you seen those times of trials as opportunities to come to Him in child-like faith and know Him as Daddy?

Write what you feel, hear, or sense from the Holy Spirit

Illustrate any pictures or scenes

He shows you

Jumping Into Revelation

The Toy on the Top Shelf

Daddy there's a toy on the top shelf I can't reach it but I want it.

Is it a gift is it for me?

I want to play with it can I have it?

Can I please play with it pleasepleaseplease?

Wow what is this it's amazing I love it how does it work?

What does it do?

Do I throw it grow it blow it or roll it?

Do I push it or pull it or paint it?

Does it fly fall flip or flash?

Does it rise hide or suprise?

Does it grow or go? Does it get up or get down?

Does it turn burn learn or discern?

Does it speed up splash down or spin around?

Daddy can You show me how it works?

Come and play with me! Daddy Daddy come *here*...

Daddy watch me! I wonder if it can do...**THIS!**

Uhh oh... Daddy...?

...can You fix it?... please?

If you then, who are evil, know how to give good gifts to your children, how much more will your Father who is in heaven give good things to those who ask him! - Matthew 7:11 (ESV)

Now they were bringing even infants to him that he might touch them. And when the disciples saw it, they rebuked them. But Jesus called them to him, saying, "Let the children come to me, and do not hinder them, for to such belongs the kingdom of God. Truly, I say to you, whoever does not receive the kingdom of God like a child shall not enter it." - Luke 18:15-17 (ESV)

At that time Jesus declared, "I thank you, Father, Lord of heaven and earth, that you have hidden these things from the wise and understanding and revealed them to little children; yes, Father, for such was your gracious will. - Matthew 11:25-26 (ESV)

Ripples:

1.) Have you seen times of trials as opportunities to come to Him as a child and know Him as Daddy?

2.) A good relationship with Daddy can be filled with wonder, excitement, joy, and innocence. When was the last time you shared in His laughter?

3.) Do you look for Him throughout your day in the brief quiet moments? He is there. Share something with Him and listen for His reply.

Write what you feel, hear, or sense from the Holy Spirit

Illustrate any pictures or scenes

He shows you

"A Walk in the Cool of the Day"

Have you ever stopped to imagine what it was like to walk with the Father soon after Creation? Not merely to picture it in your mind, but to allow yourself to experience it as if you were there in Adam or Eve's place?

"And they heard the sound of the LORD God walking in the garden in the cool of the day, and the man and his wife hid themselves from the presence of the LORD God among the trees of the garden. But the LORD God called to the man and said to him, "Where are you?" (Genesis 3:8 ESV)

It's the relaxing time of the day when the heat of the sun begins to wane and it's brightness begins to dim. My eyes see better, my ears hear better, and I begin to feel a great satisfaction for all that I've done for the day. I've been thinking of our walk all day and the time is finally nearing.

I soon hear His footsteps in the distance growing louder as He approaches. The soft earth muffles His steps but allows the sound to reach my ears with a gentle rhythm. He calls out and searches for me. I hear His whisper on the wind as if He is right next to me. Then I *know* it's time...time for my evening stroll with my *favorite* person.

Once, we heard His voice and I quickly hid behind a tree. I thought I could startle Him from behind. I waited and waited knowing He was nearby, but I must have been distracted by a squirrel or something because He came around the tree and startled me instead. I couldn't

contain my excitement to see Him and I leapt onto His back and He carried me for a while.

New discoveries overwhelm me with excitement or leave me wide-eyed and it's a struggle to remember all the questions I have for Him; there are so many fascinating things to learn and share. I'm still amazed about what I shared on yesterday's stroll, but that seems so long ago. We've been sharing our discoveries and questions for as long as I can I remember, although it hasn't been for a very long time.

I've looked forward to this part of the day as the highlight of *everything*. Working in the garden has been enjoyable and creation is fascinating, but it's *nothing* compared to spending time with Daddy. Nothing comes close to the fulfillment I have when I run to Him and

He catches me in His arms. In our last embrace I caught this amazing scent that I haven't smelled on any of the flowers so far. It's a sweet fragrance that strengthens as He moves. There's so much peace and He takes joy in hearing about all the things I've learned.

A few days ago I was smelling a beautiful flower. As I got close, an insect that looked exactly like a leaf moved. It was so sudden and I had yet to see one of those that it startled me and I fell over backward. When He saw the look on my face He laughed so hard His eyes watered.

Sometimes He shares great and exciting stories with us, but most of the time we just play and laugh together. It's the *best* part of everyday.

We are never more human than when we spend intimate time with our Father. It's what we were created for in the first place. Only one thing has changed since then, sin, but that was taken care of by Jesus. He suffered and died to restore our intimate times of playfulness with Him.

So, what is keeping *you* from an intimate time with the Father? Did you know there are many ways in which we can perceive His presence? They are all expressed in the Bible. We are still human, He still loves us, and He is still searching for us.

How many of those ways can you feel His presence? Do you hear Him, see Him, or smell His presence? When was the last time you felt His embrace or heard His laughter? When was the last time you awoke to hear the song He sings over you while you sleep? Take a few moments to ask the Father to reveal Himself to you in a way that you have not yet received Him. Look for Him today and *be ready* for a surprise visit.

Ripples:

1.) Do you look forward to spending time with God throughout the day?

2.) How many different ways can you discern His presence?

3.) What has been the most impacting declaration that the Father has spoken to you about who you are?

Write what you feel, hear, or sense from the Holy Spirit

Illustrate any pictures or scenes

He shows you

Jumping Into Revelation

Declarations: "I am"

Speak these declarations aloud. Understand these truths and take security in them. Your identity is based on who the Lord says you are. It's not based on who the world, the enemy, or even your family says you are.

"I am a child of the living God because Christ is my Lord and Savior." (John 1:12-13 ESV)

"I am cleansed of all unrighteousness through the confession of all of my sins and shortcomings" (1 John 1:9 ESV)

"I am not under condemnation, because I dwell within Him." (Romans 8:1 ESV)

"I am justified and live by the faith that belongs to the Son of God." (Galatians 2:20 ESV)

"I am crucified with Christ and my old nature has been put to death on the cross." (Romans 6:6 ESV)

"I am alive in Him, and because He lives I also live." (Romans 6:4 ESV)

"I am a new creation in Christ." (2 Corinthians 5:17 ESV)

"I am a beloved and adopted child who cries out with excitement, "Abba! Father!"" (Romans 8:15 ESV)

"I am releasing all anxiety and worry to Him. I am lifting up all needs to Him with prayers and supplications with thankfulness." (Philippians 4:6 ESV)

"I am guarded by His peace that surpasses all understanding, and my heart and mind are protected." (Philippians 4:7 ESV)

"I am a temple of the Holy Spirit." (1 Corinthians 6:19 ESV)

"I am filled to overflowing by His Spirit that lives within me." (Ephesians 5:18 ESV)

"I am one with Him through His Spirit, regardless of how I presently feel." (1 Corinthians 6:17 ESV)

"I am a unique member of the body of Christ and I have something special to offer others." (1 Corinthians 12:27, 14:26 ESV)

"I am bearing fruit as a productive branch that is connected to the vine." (John 15:5 ESV)

"I am a chosen priest and His own possession." (1 Peter 2:9 ESV)

"I am His workmanship, specifically made for His works and to do His good pleasure." (Ephesians 2:10, Philippians 2:13 ESV)

"I am a citizen of Heaven and a pilgrim in the Earth." (Philippians 3:20, Hebrews 11:13 ESV)

"I am a fearless warrior clothed in the full armor that my Father has bestowed upon me." (Ephesians 6:10-18 ESV)

"I am more than a conqueror through Him who loved me and gave Himself for me." (Romans 8:37 ESV)

"I am a friend of God." (John 15:15 ESV)

Carry these declarations with you throughout the day. Let His word and truth hold you up regardless of what the world throws at you. You're His child and dearly loved.

Ripples:

1.) What is the most impacting declaration that the Father is currently speaking to you about who you are?

2.) Are any of these declarations and views different from your current views and thoughts of yourself? If so, how?

3.) What has the enemy declared over you that needs to be cast off of you?

Write what you feel, hear, or sense from the Holy Spirit

Illustrate any pictures or scenes

He shows you

Jumping Into Revelation

Farewell to Shame

Dear Shame,

I have known you for a very long time. You were there with me through all those years of hardship. A steady companion. A trusted friend. I always knew I could count on you to be there for me when I least needed it. When I was happy, you reminded me of all the reasons I had to be sad. When I wanted to open my mouth and heart to share words with friends and siblings, you were there, standing next to me, whispering your lies and half-truths, clamping my mouth shut with your merciless hands. I know all I did wrong. You keep reminding me. But you know what? The Eternal One, the One who knows everything, HE forgave it all. He bore you for me, He carried you into the grave, He buried you with Him -
But HE arose without you.

Shame, my faithful friend,
You are dead to me

Signed: Beloved Child of the Eternal One

PS: Give your love to your mistress, bitterness.

"Take the helmet of salvation and the sword of the Spirit, which is the word of God."
    Ephesians 6:17 (NIV)

"For the word of God is living and active, sharper than any two-edged sword, piercing to the division of soul and of spirit, of joints and of marrow, and discerning the thoughts and intentions of the heart."
    Hebrews 4:12 (ESV)

Ripples:

1.) What has the enemy declared over you that you have already cast off?

2.) Are there things you would like to write a farewell letter to? Write a farewell letter/e-mail (print it out), sign it, then burn it.

3.) Who is it that releases the burden of shame?

Write what you feel, hear, or sense from the Holy Spirit

Illustrate any pictures or scenes

He shows you

My Safe Haven

When I was about 20 years old, I was enrolled as a student at a Bible school in upstate New York. I was just coming into the things of the Lord during this time and wasn't even saved yet. Even as an unbeliever though, I had an immense hunger to know and understand the Bible. I wanted to know God but hadn't truly understood salvation yet, or even understood the identity of Jesus.

During this season, I greatly battled with overcoming my personal sins and faults, but because I didn't understand the sacrifice of Christ I was trying in my own strength and self-righteousness to save myself. It wasn't even merely about "fighting the good fight," but it was almost an obsession. It grew from a healthy desire of living in holiness into a legalistic choke hold on my soul. No matter what I did, it was never good enough. No matter how hard I tried to walk in righteousness, I consistently failed and fervently condemned myself over it. It was agonizing! Knowing that we are called to be in close communion with God and yet to feel so far away from Him.

At this time I was studying the Passover in Exodus 12. The image of the blood on the door posts was firmly placed in my mind. I continued to think about how comforting it must have been to know that because of the protection of the blood you would be safe from the wrath to come. I pondered over these thoughts time and time again. I have always had a fascination with the word of God. I've always been drawn to read His word and to delve deeper and deeper into it, and to try and grow closer to Him through studying it.

One night, I was reading the scriptures and studying the ancient Greek of the New Testament. I was reading one of the most well-known and most often recited verses in the entire Bible: John 3:16. I read through it with an almost casual air about me. I thought to myself, "Yeah, I already know what this verse says. You'd have to be living under a rock to not know what John 3:16 says!" But as I read over this supposedly familiar verse in a literal translation of the Greek, I was struck by the difference of just one word. The difference of just one word can change *everything*!

While most know this verse and recite it as such,

"For God so loved the world, that he gave his only begotten Son, that whosoever believeth in him should not perish, but have everlasting life." (KJV)

This literal translation had one word *changed* that ended up *changing* me for forever!

It read,

"For God so loved the world, that he gave his only begotten Son, that whosoever believeth into him should not perish, but have everlasting life."

Did you catch it? Instead of saying "believeth in Him," it says "believeth *into* Him." I did a double take. I thought, "That must be a typo or some kind of an error!" I checked in the Greek and sure enough it *was* the word "*into*!" "So what?!" Exclaims some skeptic. "In! Into! It's the same thing! It makes no difference!" Well, let me tell you, rhetorical heckler, it absolutely does make a difference! It makes all the difference in the world!

Believing "*in*" something can be much like believing in a creed or a doctrine. It's merely agreement that something is true and that you accept it as true, but to believe "*into*" something is quite different. For example, if I wished to use an elevator, how ridiculous would I look if I simply stood outside of the elevator and kept declaring, "I believe in this elevator!"? People would think I was nuts! If I truly believed in the elevator and trusted the elevator, I would believe myself into it. In other words, if I truly believed in it and trusted it, I would show that faith by entering into it and allowing it to carry me where I needed to go. The same thing happened for me and this particular verse.

The moment I realized that "*into*" was what was actually implied, it all hit me at once! Just like the Passover and the blood over the door post, as the Israelites believed into the promises of God by faith they entered into the safe haven that the blood offered for them within their dwelling places. Christ *is* that safe haven! We don't need to strive, and struggle, and battle to implement our own self-righteousness. We simply need to accept the safe haven of Jesus Christ and understand that it is He who covers us! It is Christ that keeps us safe! It is Christ who bears the weight and burden of our sin! It is Christ who imputes His righteousness to us so that we don't have to trust in our imperfect strength! As that revelation went deep into my spirit, it was then that I came alive to Christ. That was the night that I got saved and finally understood what it means to have Christ as Savior.

    That night the weight and burden of sin left me and I felt light as a feather. I couldn't believe the freedom that I had found in Him. He was my safe haven and continues to be so to this day!

Ripples:

1.) Who is it that releases the burden of shame, especially the shame of self-righteousness?

2.) Why do you think that many are more willing to trust in their own righteousness over the righteousness of Christ?

3.) Life-changing revelation can come through the Word as well as through dreams. What dreams have you had where you believe the Lord was speaking to you?

Write what you feel, hear, or sense from the Holy Spirit

Illustrate any pictures or scenes

He shows you

Jumping Into Revelation

Theme Park Heaven

The word of God reveals to us that,

"It is the glory of God to conceal things, but the glory of kings is to search things out." Proverbs 25:2 (ESV)

The Lord conceals some revelation in certain places that are harder to reach. When He does this we must seek Him more consistently and more earnestly to discover it. The results are greater revelation of Himself and a more intimate connection with Him. In this manner He invites us into deeper relationship and with this comes an increase of the revelation of His glory.

When we search out the things He has concealed for us, we are exercising the authority He gave us in a "kingly" manner. I invite you to walk in this authority and discover what the King of Kings has to say to His kings. Search out the meaning the Lord has concealed in this dream for you to discover.

If you have concerns for the source of dreams or their purpose in this application, I invite you to turn to the Appendix for our views on these matters.

In a dream, Jesus told me a parable about **ants that built a tower 150 feet high**. I shared this parable with my children and we would witness it shortly afterward. Our journey began by walking across a path of ice over a pool of water. We traveled to a plot of land in the south where there was a theme park based on this parable.

I saw what looked like a high definition cartoon of ants building a tower 150 feet high. I took pictures of this place with my phone and later retold what I saw to a **little boy with blonde hair**. He was the son of a nationally known pastor I was listening to at the time of this dream. This pastor confirmed my teaching by stating the reference of the passage the parable was found in; he said it was in **Matthew 7**.

As I recounted to the boy, I relived the experience again. I showed him three pictures: one of a huge tree, another of a red barn sitting on a 40 foot high stone riser that was 20 feet higher, and lastly, a picture of a tree stump that was about 15' wide.

In the next scene we were back in a high definition cartoon in which **ants were crossing the road**. They were moving a 150 foot stalk of grass into their theme park from across the road where they had cultivated it. We were amazed at how tall 150 feet was and how well they moved the stalk. We understood this to be an example of how tall 150 feet really was.

It was time to enter the theme park, so we climbed the 150 foot tower up to its lobby. The lobby was decorated in elaborately rich detail. As we walked its walkways, safety barriers and pathways unfolded before us as we moved. Bricks and stones moved and shifted before us to bring us further into a castle and it felt much like home.

The **owner of the castle** welcomed us from our journey and encouraged us to enjoy ourselves. There weren't many people up here so it was not very busy. The atmosphere was extremely peaceful.

Further in the distance we noticed several roller coasters. They were 150 feet long and extremely fast. On one you placed skates on your feet and stepped on a double rail and it zipped you along the track in just a few seconds. My son, who *also* has blond hair, was there and we watched him strap in and zip out of sight in a second. I chased after him laughing. We met up with him at the end of the ride. I meditated on this dream awhile before I became fully awake.

Tools for Interpretation:

"And the waters prevailed on the earth 150 days" Gen. 7:24 (ESV)

Remember what Solomon said about the ant in Proverbs 6:6 and 30:25?

What does a tower represent in the Bible?

What message do you suppose the young boy was learning by the three pictures?

Read through Matthew 7 and note connections.

Why do you suppose we had to watch the ants cross the road?

Ripples:

1.) Who was the owner of the castle that greeted us?

2.) What example does the older boy provide for us?

3.) What do you discern is the overall message of this dream?

Write what you feel, hear, or sense from the Holy Spirit

Illustrate any pictures or scenes He shows you

Jumping Into Revelation

Deep Dive: John 3:8

"The wind blows where it wishes, and you hear its sound, but you do not know where it comes from or where it goes. So it is with everyone who is born of the Spirit." - John 3:8 ESV

On a particular night, a lone Pharisee by the name of Nicodemus sought out a certain preacher that had been a thorn in the side of the religious elite: Jesus of Nazareth. He came under the cover of darkness since the Pharisees had openly opposed Jesus and His teachings, and it probably wasn't the wisest decision for him or his reputation to be seen conversing with this pariah in a non-hostile manner.

He came to Jesus. Jesus received him.

From the very beginning of the discussion he openly admits to Christ that he and his sect are well aware of Whom Jesus is and Who has commissioned Him for this ministry. Jesus evades his comments and goes straight for the jugular, declaring, "Truly, truly, I say to you, unless one is born again he cannot see the kingdom of God" (3:3). Nicodemus is beyond perplexed. His mind is so entirely absorbed in this natural world that that is all he can relate this statement to. "Can one possibly enter into his mother's womb a second time and be born again?!?! This doesn't make any sense!"

Even though this is among the first steps of one's spiritual journey, it is still a heavy burden for Nicodemus' worldly mind to attempt to comprehend. Jesus takes him a step further. He shows him that spiritual birth comes through water and spirit, and exposits on the principle of natures producing after their own kind. At this point Nicodemus probably had an expression of absolute confusion on his face. "Don't marvel that I've told you these things!" Christ was merely explaining the elementary concepts of the spiritual life.

After carefully taking his guest step-by-step through these teachings, he finally hits at the heart of walking and living in the spirit in verse eight. Many know this verse and have read it in its usual symbolic form. The blowing of the wind is a simple enough analogy to explain the workings of the spirit, and even fits in with the usual parabolic style of Jesus' teachings, but it seems somewhat out of place in this specific instance. Jesus is teaching a curious individual about the ways of the Spirit of God and expounding to him of its importance. Wouldn't it make sense for Him to say as much? Well, He does. When we look at the ancient Greek we can see this text in a more straightforward manner. Let's dive into the original Greek of the text!

The amazing thing about Greek is that it's an incredibly detailed language that can have a number of meanings or nuances even within individual words. The astonishing fact of this particular verse is that it can be accurately translated in one of two different ways! The first is the usual translation that many of us have heard since our youth, while the other is one that isn't often heard of. By looking at the alternate translation of some keywords we are able to see the other side of the textual coin.

The word for spirit is "*Pneuma*," which can be translated as "*wind*," or it can also be translated as "*spirit*." So, Jesus *was* blatantly speaking about the Spirit in this verse! Next, the word "*Pnei*" for "blow" can also be translated as "*breathe*." It can mean blowing, just like the wind, or it can mean to breathe or exhale. Lastly, the word for "*sound*," the Greek word "*Phone*," can also be accurately translated into English as "*voice*."

By taking these other definitions into account, we are able to see that Jesus could have been very cleverly using these specific words to give a two-fold picture. In the first, we have the analogy of the wind. In the second, we have a more direct approach. A literal alternate translation could read as such,

"The Spirit breathes where it desires, and you hear its voice, but you do not know where it comes from or where it goes. So it is with everyone who is born of the Spirit."

By translating it in this manner it ties in more smoothly with the ending portion that speaks of those who have been born of this nature. Isn't the word of God incredible! This imagery paints a vivid picture of the normal Christian life.

    The Spirit shows up on the scene unexpectedly! He breathes into specific situations and into specific people's lives. We don't fully understand where He came from, where He's going, or what He's always up to, but we still recognize that still small voice and follow it wherever it goes. It's beautiful! This is what we were created for, and this is why the Spirit birthed us into this life in Christ: for His good pleasure!

Ripples:

1.) How does this further understanding of John 3:8 affect you personally? Does it encourage you to seek out the Spirit more?

2.) Is there anything in your life that you think could be hindering you from hearing the voice of God clearly? Ask the Lord to remove all hindrances from you and to give you ears to hear what the Spirit is speaking to you, in Jesus' name.

3.) The Lord conceals a matter so that the wise may search it out, while the enemy seeks to hide matters for the purpose of deception. Is there something that you're currently attempting to hide?

Write what you feel, hear, or sense from the Holy Spirit

Illustrate any pictures or scenes

He shows you

The Masquerade Invitation

You are cordially invited to a

Masquerade Ball

Pre-Approved!

Theme: "Carpe Diem."
"Take a break from your life and feel free to lose yourself."

Time: May 6th at 22:13 (10:13 pm)

Venue: Sapphira's Lot

Location: 1313 2nd Sam Circle, Adullam

Conditions: Find a mask, wear it well, so none of us can see and tell

Attire: Dress to impress

Food: Eidolothuton. Absolutely no fruit!

I received this strange invitation in the mail. Its wording was a little odd and I didn't recognize the location. To be honest, it seemed a bit ominous. I couldn't help but notice the bright colors splashing across the front, and the promise of pre-approval on the envelope. Pre-approval... That's like pre-acceptance, right? They would accept me for me, pre-existing conditions and all. Excitement entered my heart, and it skipped a beat. I have actually been invited to a *party*! They didn't care who I was, what happened to me, or what I've done. There's no disapproval for those that wear a mask. It doesn't matter if I deserve it or not, I've already been pre-accepted, pre-approved.

I couldn't wait to show this amazing invitation to my best friend. We would have such a great time, but I was taken aback by her reaction. Instead of wanting to go with me, she tried to talk me out of going!
I asked her, "Don't you want to have fun? Don't you want to take a break from your life for a little while, to stop being yourself and not worry what other people may think? This is an invitation to a party where we'll be unconditionally loved!"
She said that I didn't belong with those people and that I shouldn't attend. She said that they really didn't care about me, they just cared about themselves and what I might bring or do to make them look better. I became furious with her and

left. Some of my acquaintances saw me leaving her house. I showed them the invitation and they got one too and said they would be going. I can't wait!

The Aftermath

I got home late last night. The party was not what I expected! Throughout the night I danced and sang, I shouted and I ate my fill. I was living a dream. There was no pain. No shame. Nothing to be afraid of and nothing to hold me back. As the midnight hour approached, confidence in my new self deepened as the urge to reveal my true heart grew. If these people love me like this, maybe they will love me with the mask off too.
As I anticipated the first bell of the midnight hour, I was so excited to hear it that I removed my mask with a heartfelt shout, but the stroke never came. As I looked around, no one else took their masks off; it was still 11:59. Everyone gasped as they saw my true self. I didn't know that they would respond that way. It was a party after all. But they rejected me. They shunned me. Some of them hurt me as I was forced to leave. All of my acquaintances who were there never spoke a word in my defense.
As I made my way home, I saw my friend who told me not to go to the party; she saw my hurt, she saw my pain, she saw what the people at the party did to me. My friend loved me and comforted me in my brokenness. She never left my side as we cried together all night. She were right. I didn't belong at

that party because my true self is much more precious than any mask I could ever wear."

Invitation Explanation

- An invitation to you to hide your flaws, sins, shame, or pain does not come from the Father. He takes you where you, heals, cleanses and strengthens.
- A focus on living in the moment with little to no thought for the future (theme)
- Isa. 22:12-13 (date/time)
- Acts 5, 2 Peter 2:8 (venue)
- 2 Sam. 13:13, 1 Sam. 22:1 (location)
- Greek word for idol sacrifice (food)

Ripples:

1.) What if *you* received this invitation in the mail?

2.) Would you go or would you heed the advice of your friend, even if it doesn't sound like what you want to hear?

3.) Would you attend, being driven by your curiosity or would it be the desire to be free

and loved that leads you into the company
of these strangers?

Write what you feel, hear, or sense from the Holy Spirit

Illustrate any pictures or scenes

He shows you

Jumping Into Revelation

A Brother's Plea

Dear Family,

I write to you in love, but I'm afraid the news isn't all good. Things are far worse than it seemed, and it continues to grow worse.

Our dearly departed brother needs our support and prayers desperately! He has given into the ways of this world, and what started as a little compromise has led to ruination. The enemy now has him in a choke hold, and what life was there is now fading fast! With each demand he falls farther into the Devil's trap, and soon he will surrender all control and the Devil will have complete domination over him!

His words are no longer his own for the enemy is after that too. Words that once brought me comfort now sound sweet in my ear, but taste bitter in my soul. Our Father resides in him no longer, for the enemy is the one whom he now listens to! Though his foundation used to be built in stone, he now builds a house of cards on shifting sand!!

His house is now in ruins, but is held up by popularity; full of flashing lights and shiny stained glass.
I urge you please to join together in prayer for our dear brother, our brother the church!

Brothers and sisters in Christ, we must join together now, and put aside our differences, for the salvation of the world is at stake!!!

Though I be guilty of turning a blind eye to this, I can do so no longer! I am bound to the truth of the gospel, and though I may be ridiculed, beaten, imprisoned, or even killed, I must release the burning word God has placed on my heart! I urge you all to join me. Though it will cost me my life, I consider it a joy to lay it down, that our

lost brothers and sisters may find out the truth, and come back home.

**Much love,
your brother in Christ**

Ripple Questions:

1.) The masquerade only goes so far, it's time for the face to face talk with Father. Is there something you've kept hidden?

2.) What pattern of this world are you most vulnerable to?

3.) What is stronger, the pattern of this world or who He created you to be?

Write what you feel, hear, or sense from the Holy Spirit

Illustrate any pictures or scenes

He shows you

In Ageless Wonder

We've all been there at one time or another. Feeling beat up, worn out, and exhausted.

Feeling old on the inside while still young on the outside. It's as if our souls reflect an age 20 years beyond our physical age.

There are a number of reasons we can feel this.

Sometimes we were given responsibilities beyond our capability and it caused us to grow up quicker than we should have.

We develop an independence that causes us to miss out on a childhood that we can never get back.

We grieve our loss and feel like opportunities were missed that we will never be able to reclaim.

Some of us try to relive our childhood well beyond the appropriate years, and thus, stunt our maturity long after we would have attained it in its proper timing.

Independence and immaturity are never a good mix because what once toughened us so we could survive now just isolates us from others.

Those that could help are not allowed to and...

A cycle is born, a pattern forms, and the seasons spin on...

Sometimes it comes at the hands of an abuser.

We've been placed into a position where we have had to endure emotional or physical affliction before we were mature enough to understand what was happening to us.

These scars run deeply into our soul, inflicting harm on an innocence that hinders freedoms that only children experience.

Now, they rob us of sensitivity needed to enjoy freedoms that healthy adults enjoy.

Frustration and anger, at times, rise to the surface and we harm an innocent person we feel safe with.

Hoping they do not retaliate and give us what we deserve, we keep them under control and...

A cycle is born, a pattern forms, and the seasons spin on...

Sometimes we do it to ourselves. We engage in self abuse because we believe that it is better to experience a fleeting pleasure than the weight of our own mistakes and poor choices.

After the pleasure has passed, we notice the weight has increased.

We've added a sin on top of a sin.

We feel the increased pressure restricting our ability to move, to breath, to be our true self.

We know better, but that little bit of pleasure draws us in for another taste that promises us the ability to forget the former for a few more fleeting moments and...

A cycle is born, a pattern forms, and the seasons spin on...

I know what you're thinking.

You think the problem is you.

You're stuck in this cycle, this pattern, and the seasons are flying by. You think it's your own fault and the shame is crushing you.

You blame your parents, your friends, your children in hopes that they will make a change what will release you from this cycle.

When they can't make the changes you need you must make a choice: do you remind them of their need to change or take responsibility for what you know deep down is yours?

When you decide to take responsibility I quickly rush to your side and encourage you with words of life.

That feeling you get when you know you can make the change?

That's Me working with you, closer than you thought I could be.

That tingle you feel on your hand?

That's Me holding yours.

The warmth you feel in your chest?

That's my love's embrace.

This will never change, I will always be at your side when you take responsibility for your sins and mistakes.

We've been here before, haven't we?

You have tried to change many times with little success, despite My presence, despite My grace.

You fight hard for a little while, but the battle is intense and the progress is small.

Discouragement washes over you and you quit, falling back and...

A cycle is born, a pattern forms, and the seasons spin on...

You think this to is your fault, but it's time I let you in on a secret. Draw close My child and listen to My words. Come sit on my lap so you can feel My love while I instruct you on the way things work.

You are trying to change the wrong things. You fight to break the patterns, reverse the cycles, and rearrange the seasons.

That is not a fight you can win, because it's not a fight you are supposed to have.

Cycles, patterns, and seasons are the things of the world.

It is the way the world moves. The earth laps around the sun, days and nights dance in tandem, seasons spin about, time is measured in repeating patterns.

I do not exist in time, in cycles, patterns, or seasons. I Am in ageless wonder and I created you to be like Me.

I did not create you to move in cycles, patterns and seasons.

When you move in the ways of the world, when you flow within it's channels you will become stuck in it pathways.

Changing the cycles, patterns and seasons is like trying to change the way the world works.

Ha ha, My child, I love your spirit of adventure and the desire to take on the world, but you didn't create it. You are not able to change the way it works, especially while following its courses.

I created you to be like Me, in ageless wonder and pattern free. Your body moves in patterns because it belongs to this world, but your spirit, given by Me, is always pattern free.

Rise up, My child, from the patterns of this world, rise up to the place you were created to be! You sit above the world and all it's ways, in ageless wonder, right beside Me.

Ephesians 2:1-7

"And you were dead in the trespasses and sins [2] in which you once walked, following the course of this world, following the prince of the power of the air, the spirit that is now at work in the sons of disobedience-- [3] among whom we all once lived in the passions of our flesh, carrying out the desires of the body and the mind, and were by nature children of wrath, like the rest of mankind. [4] But God, being rich in mercy, because of the great love with which he loved us, [5] even when we were dead in our trespasses, made us alive together with Christ -by grace you have been saved-- [6] and raised us up with him and seated us with him in the heavenly places in Christ Jesus, [7] so that in the coming ages he might show the immeasurable riches of his grace in kindness toward us in Christ Jesus."

Ripple Questions:

1.) What pattern of this world have you been falling into this past year?

2.) How strong is the authority given to you through Christ?

3.) What do you turn to when in doubt your authority?

Write what you feel, hear, or sense from the Holy Spirit

Illustrate any pictures or scenes

He shows you

Jumping Into Revelation

What is Real

When all my rivers have run dry
When my soul is weary from the road
When my wings are too heavy to fly
And my shoulders are stooped from the load
I call upon Your name.

When all that's left of a roaring fire
Are dying embers and tired flames
When all the world cares about is my attire
And I'm sick of playing all their twisted games
I grasp for what is real.

When life's storms have left me broken and bent
When my dreams are scattered around like debris
When my feet are leaden and my breath is spent
When love is dead and hope has abandoned me
I cling to Your hand.

When the lights have gone out and darkness surrounds
When wolves howl in the distance and nightmares are set loose
When I've fallen into the pit and despair abounds
When death is closing in and my necklace is a noose
I cry out to You.

When the night is at its end
And the sky is turning gray
All my wounds I know You'll mend
As ev'ry shadow fades away
I praise Your name.

Ripples:

1.) List three ways you take authority over worldly patterns.

2.) It's the midnight hour, will you praise Him?

3.) Will you praise Him through the most frightening of life-threatening circumstances?

Write what you feel, hear, or sense from the Holy Spirit

Illustrate any pictures or scenes

He shows you

Jumping Into Revelation

Cancer

Cancer is a scary word. When one first hears it, they often think for the worst, sometimes even the end. In my life personally, I understand this word all to well.

In the young years of my life, when most were learning to play catch and singing their ABC's, I was fighting a battle for life, one that leukemia was fighting to take away from me. This battle continued on strongly in my life for almost 20 years. Now most of you may be thinking 20 years seems like an awfully long battle, but truthfully it was only fought physically for 3 ½ of those years, however, I felt like I was battling it in my mind for 17 more years after that.

The truth is I held on to it, turning it into a prison cell in which seemed to be no escape! The fear that I could no longer live a normal life, fear of dreaming, or being able to do normal things again became overpowering. Looking over my shoulder at every turn with a fear that it would once again find me and take over my life, but this time with no escape! Truthfully, I was living as though I had already died.

In our lives, cancer can take on many forms, and often times it isn't in the physical as we all imagine it. It can come in the form of doubt, fears, or hurtful words from others, often those we care about the most. When it comes down to it, the enemy doesn't have to harm us to keep us from doing the will of God, it's really as simple as planting a seed of doubt. If you allow the devil a foothold in your mind, it can be all that's necessary to keep you where you are now, reflecting on your past, rather than moving forward into all that God has planned for your life.

    A few years ago, God rocked my world as I knew it, by asking me to go to a 3rd world country I had never heard of till that time, and to do something that was definitely out of my comfort zone! Till that time I had never had any plans or dreams of travel, because I was still stuck in fear of the unknown. Even though I was still skeptical, I went, even though I had no idea where I was going.

    Half way through that trip, something unexpected happened! While on our way back from the mountains, our bus broke down leaving us on the side of the road, miles from help, and out of any form of communication range. Though on one side I knew we would be ok, but on the other it was a representation of my life: stuck in one place, going nowhere in life, and not in good communication with the Father.

    After an hour on the road we were back up and heading for the city, however, sitting in my seat I felt like I was in a prison. On the outside I seemed OK, but inside I was falling apart and crying out to God to change my thinking and to release me from the bondage I seemed to be in. But then God happened! A group of people came over and asked how I was doing, and for the first time I opened up my heart and I shared my fear and feeling of being stuck in a box. The team gathered around me and began praying, and immediately the Holy Spirit showed up and began ministering to me. I felt a HUGE weight fall off of my shoulders, so much so that I felt if I opened my eyes and looked through the tears I would see a large pile of logging chains lying on the floor of the bus!

      For the first time I felt freedom from my fears, and for the first time in almost 20 years I felt alive! That night I said, "No more Satan! I am a child of God, and I know He has a plan for my life that is far from the fears of my past!" God began to give me dreams and visions of the future and what He had in store for me. What seemed like a small step and a few words became one of the greatest, most impacting moments of my life! One where I left my past behind, left it in God's hands, and opened my life to Him to use for His purpose and glory.

Genesis 12:1

2 Timothy 1:7

2 Corinthians 3:17

John 8:36

Psalm 118:5

Luke 4:18

Ripple Questions:

1.) What fears from your past are trapping you from your destiny?

2.) If cancer was a spirit that attacked your identity what would be its name?

3.) Who are you according what the Father says about you?

Write what you feel, hear, or sense from the Holy Spirit

Illustrate any pictures or scenes

He shows you

Dear Self-Doubt

Dear Self-Doubt,

I hear your words as I fall asleep, about things I've done
Each word a dagger stinging the flesh and cutting my soul
You fill my night with dreams in exchange for my own
Uncertainty filling me with constant words that take a toll

I hear your words as I awake, about the things I will face
Each word a weight, slowing my walk to a troubled stagger
Fearing failure and failing to risk when you oppose my grace
Oppressing me by the mark I missed and calling me a laggard

Self-Doubt, you are a thief with no identity of your own
You want my gifts, you want my favor, you want my purpose
You want my soil, you want my sun, and the seeds I've sown

But these are not mine to keep and they are not mine to lose

See, my Dad, He tells me who I am and He beckons me to sit
On a throne at His right hand, far above you and all your kind
Through Jesus He assigned me grace, for you He assigned the pit
Everlasting love in the ages to come as I am His and He is mine

Ripples:

1.) How are cancer of the body and self-doubt to identity similar?

2.) What the enemy has tried to take from you is what he most fears you will use against him. Use it by saying it aloud and declaring it over yourself.

3.) Today, you will be given the opportunity to use it to overcome the enemy and give glory to God, watch for your opportunity.

Write what you feel, hear, or sense from the Holy Spirit

Illustrate any pictures or scenes

He shows you

Jumping Into Revelation

Jumping Into Revelation

A Cry From Atop

Love　　　　　gone　**wild**
Slipping into <u>***unforgettable***</u>
Never forgetting

Every **friend** held dear　　　　Till the very last breath

Some say it's <u>***failure***</u>　　　　Love never
bails

Not always **present**　　　　**But** always *there*

Held fast to the eternal Truths

Wretched in the [p|r|i|s|o|n] of *Flesh*

Cursed to the Earth from Birth

<u>**There is no escape**</u>

149

Jumping Into Revelation

It's the sweet aroma chased

                         Some hide it well

Others see no reason to hide

                         It's all been done

Nothing new

                         Fostering dreams of change

      Whispers   in   the   wind

Chasing after time

        Grasping at nothing

            Creating castles of circles

                  Lands for the selfish to cry in vain

              The vanities become the truths

Hearing Words filtered through self

The delusions
become a reality
The Crazy   *calling the shots*
The Lost   *become the leader*

Jumping Into Revelation

       It is the History telling the future
           Happy when Seeing the smiles
        Quirky grins in memories
Of all that have gone ahead

The 3 cord strands hold strong

Binding as Spirit testifies to Spirit

The things seen may not be

           What is to be done?

Lost in the blinders

           What is it you think you see?

A business format set to fail

          Hear if you have ears
          See if you have eyes

Jumping Into Revelation

For worldly loss
Is great Gain
Money and fame will be
Your only reward

For the treasures
Are the Spirits of
All you have come to see

So what is it you want to be?

It's a cry in the wilderness
Making a way

The visions of the people pushed
To the ground
And stolen from atop

Jumping Into Revelation

The platforms built to set above
Seeing progress through levels
Cursed is the ground of the proud
For falling is a fear too great to bare
Scared hiding behind the walls
Built to hide and protect
The dwellings on earth
All work will be lost

Reward is in the mirror

For internal is the place of the Kingdom

Who knows a man's struggle

Judging on the wisdom of the world

Chasing will be your reward

Left behind in the castles of delusion

Wreckage and disaster await

The castle you seek

Is a pile of rubble

When seen through love

Ripples:

1.) What line in this word speaks to you most?

2.) Do you see any patterns in the poetry? What do you think the patterns pertain to with the meaning of each line?

3.) When in your life has the Lord brought order out of chaos, and peace out of turmoil?

Write what you feel, hear, or sense from the Holy Spirit

Illustrate any pictures or scenes

He shows you

Jumping Into Revelation

A Warning Dream

"When I say, 'My bed will comfort me, my couch will ease my complaint,' then you scare me with dreams and terrify me with visions."

Job 7:13-14 ESV

I arrived late at the night to a house that was two stories high. I *climbed a ladder* to the top of the second floor, where the third floor would have been if there was one. I stepped over the wall and came down inside of the second floor the house. There was a door right behind the ladder that I could have used and I realized I didn't have to climb over. I could have just come through that door.

I recognized the lady of the house as my *Life Insurance Salesperson*. I arrived at *12 am* and was in a hurry because I knew that I needed to be up around *2:30 am for work*. I needed her to put *makeup* on me and her service would cost *$14.50*.

The Life Insurance Salesperson was not in a hurry to work on me. She just laid back down to go to sleep. I tried to wake her so she could put on my makeup, but said *she wouldn't serve me*. I asked my spouse, who was with me now, if she could do it instead. I explained to my spouse that I just wanted to cover up the blemishes. She took notice of my hair instead, and that the sides were really long. I really looked bad with blemishes and long lopsided hair. She took barber shears and quickly *chopped through my hair*. She cut it almost all the way down but left the top. I looked in the mirror and saw that I now had a weird mohawk and I looked ridiculous.

Jumping Into Revelation

The Interpretation of The Warning Dream

Climbing the Ladder - I'm striving in my own power to come into God's presence (3rd heaven) but this cannot be done in our own power. Our own power gets us to the 2nd heaven where evil spirits rule. See 2 Corinthians 12:2 and Ephesians 6:12.

The Insurance Salesperson - They symbolize the aspect of the Holy Spirit that insures your life if tragedy should strike. The Spirit won't serve those that seek their own gain to feed their pride. See 2 Corinthians 1:22, Eph. 1:13, and 4:30.

Makeup - This is used to cover blemishes and impurities on the skin that others won't notice. I'm not coming to the Spirit in repentance for sin to be washed or cleansed away, but to conceal my blemishes and cover my face. This is an unrepentant heart that is concerned with the way man perceives my identity. This is to live a lie instead of confessing and repenting of sin.

She Wouldn't Serve Me - The Holy Spirit won't aid a prideful person that will not repent. We can't ask for the empowerment of the Holy Spirit while seeking to cover up and hide our sins.

Time of Arrival - 12am is the time given when we are to seek the Lord. It can be a time of deliverance or disaster depending upon the condition of your heart when you approach Him. I came with selfish intentions, not for the benefit of others. See Luke 11:5-10 and Acts 16:25-26.

Time to Depart for Work - 2:30am. It is time to come into agreement with God's ministry for my life.

2 means to come into agreement. See Amos 3:3 and Matt. 18:18.

30 is the symbol for serving Jesus completely. See Lev. 1:7 and 2 Sam 5:4. On a related note, Jesus was baptized and entered into His ministry at 30 years old.

The Cost of $14.50 - 14 is the number for deliverance or disaster. See Acts 27:27-44 and Ex. 12:6-36

50 is the number for Jubilee, which is to say all debts are paid and you are set free to experience the full measure of your inheritance. See Lev. 25:10. When we come to the Father with a repentant heart He delivers us because our debts were already paid in the name of Jesus. See Luke 7:43-48. If instead we desire to conceal our sins or hide our flaws so we can continue in them, disaster awaits us.

Quickly Chopped Through My Hair - Having your haircut in a dream is a symbol for being humbled for breaking a vow. The result is the Holy Spirit lifts His anointing from you until you repent and become humble. See Judges 16:16-22.

When it comes to dreams, all warnings are good warnings. The Father does not want disaster to fall upon us, but rather that we experience the fullness of every one of His amazing blessings.

If we are in sin, He wants us to turn from sin back to Him.

If we are headed toward dangerous ground, He wants us to realign our direction back to the path He has marked out for us.

If we are following our pride and hiding our flaws rather than repenting, disaster awaits us.

Turn to Him, He is waiting for you...waiting for your response.

>*If you have any concerns about the source of dreams or their purpose in this application, I invite you to turn to the appendix for our views on these matters. See Appendix

Write what you feel, hear, or sense from the Holy Spirit

Illustrate any pictures or scenes

He shows you

Jumping Into Revelation

The Chair

Sitting staring into a blank oblivion
I see the dream of me
Everyone laughing and singing with glee
Carrying me on my chair
On the walls are dramatic pictures of me
But this is never to be

For I am sitting strapped to a chair
All the fingers pointing
Wandered off in dreams
While the beast wistfully slips through
The cracks in the fortress of my spirit
Killing everything I have learned to love

Still sitting in this silent dark room
To my knees is where I'm meant to be
A crack in the shield
Sitting eating at the table with glee
Catching the drool on my knee
Eyes blank with pain
And filled with fight
Am I a Knight?

Crying in this room...is it day or night?
Fear is only a distant comfort
Can't see past these illusions of grandeur
Waiting to shift into 6th
They may not be ready...yet
I'm frozen to this heated seat
Am I missing the entire fight?

Past mountains of profession

Jumping Into Revelation

Pronouncing the pouncing lions
Presence

Climbed and conquered so much
No glory or fame
Given to the undeserving
It's a shame to see the wisdom of the world
Working in the scenery of the Kingdom
Infiltrated from the inside patterns of structure
Running back to the comfort zone of the standard
Too afraid to push to the front
Knowing you may just get what you want
The faith is so strong no one can break the concentration
The trust wavers from the inside
Know but testing the waters
Falling back to wisdom and waiting
When He calls us to Run and He will guide our steps
The scaffolding of man falls under attack
The Knees of God will never bow
Slipping from this chair I fall to my knees
Liking a raging bulldog the fluids fly
As I present my disgust of myself
For doing so much
But nothing at all

Ripples:

1.) Have you ever felt so trapped in the darkest hour that you wanted to scream out loud in frustration?

2.) When the moment to fight back against the enemy comes and you see through the lies, do you make sure that you are relying upon the Holy Spirit or do you lash out in your own strength?

3.) Sometimes in our darkest hour we can feel like we're wandering alone with nowhere to go and no place to call home. Where do we seek hope and where can we find solace?

Write what you feel, hear, or sense from the Holy Spirit

Illustrate any pictures or scenes He shows you

Jumping Into Revelation

The Sojourner

The pilgrim marches across the lands.
He seeks a kingdom not made with hands.
He burns his feet on the scorching sands.
This is all there ever is.

He trudges through the muck and mire,
Seeking for a holy fire.
Facing man's enduring ire.
This is all there ever is.

He knows the light resides somewhere
In a realm of sacred prayer
Where a lord gives solemn care.
This is all there ever is.

This race self-seeking serves its own,
And hates the pilgrim, cause unknown.
He goes his way without a groan.
This is all there ever is.

A scroll he reads pertaining to life
Strikes his heart like a sharpened knife.
Cleansing his heart of every strife.
Is this all there ever is?

He follows the way. He walks the path.
Forsaking sadness, leaving wrath.
The world can't see the aftermath.
Is this all there ever is?

He sees a hill crowned with a tree,
A blood-soaked man in agony.
"My God, have you forsaken Me?"
Is this the lord Who ever lives?

Lord who's a lion and a lamb.
He calls Himself the Great I AM.
He bears the weight of the damned.
He is all there ever is.

Ripples:

1.) What moments of peace have you found in your pilgrim wanderings in this life? What has been your greatest solace?

2.) How do the lines at the end of each stanza pertain to the Sojourner's travels? Do you see a progression, and what does that mean to you?

3.) Although the sojourner was able to easily ignore the judgment of the world, not all of us handle that kind of treatment so well. What have been some of the reactions that you've had when you've faced persecution for your Christian walk?

Write what you feel, hear, or sense from the Holy Spirit

Illustrate any pictures or scenes

He shows you

Prison Release

Released, but sin-conscious

The day I was first released started like any other day. The cold, dark cell with only a small barred window for light was all I had ever known. All at once the prison door was thrown open and Jesus stood before me dressed in white. He then beckoned me to come out of the prison with him. I took his hand and walked out of the prison completely free. Not far from the prison stood a crowd of people all looking and pointing at me and I suddenly became aware that I was still dressed in my prison clothes.
A few months later I had the same dream, except this time I wasn't self-conscious about what I was wearing after I was released, and instead of the prison clothes that I had formerly been dressed in, I was now all dressed in white.

The Revelation

The first dream represented when I and others like me became free, we still felt defined by our sin and not by Jesus. The second dream was the freedom that comes from the identity of being a son which was represented by being dressed all in white like Jesus.

Jumping Into Revelation

Ripples:

1.) What differences or similarities are there between suffering for your faith and suffering for your past?

2.) What kind of stereotypical boxes have others tried to put you into in the past?

3.) Do you let the journey of your past define who you are now?

Write what you feel, hear, or sense from the Holy Spirit

Illustrate any pictures or scenes

He shows you

Jumping Into Revelation

The Journey of Hope: A True Story of Damage, Darkness, and Forgiveness Part One

Once upon a time, there lived a young girl named Hope. She lived with her family in a small village about a day's ride from the city. Her mother and father were leaders in their church, her best friend was her elder sister, and her aunt lived with them too. Everyone was quite happy there. Most of all, Hope loved to dance in worship for her Lord and Savior, Jesus Christ. But their happiness did not last very long, for soon a terrible darkness fell over their land.

Hope's aunt had married a man with evil intentions. When her mother and father went to converse with the other leaders of their church once a month, her aunt and new uncle would come to look after Hope and her sister. Unbeknownst to anyone, Hope's new uncle took advantage of her in the most intimate way possible. He gently violated her so that no one would suspect anything amiss, especially Hope. Since she was so young, she did not know it was wrong for a family member to touch her in that way. This practice of sexual molestation continued for many months until she finally told her mother. Hope was still unaware of the wrong that was being done to her, and she wondered why her mother looked so shocked and terrified upon hearing of her uncle's actions.

A private meeting was held between their two church pastors, Hope's father, and her uncle to determine if these accusations were true. Denial was her uncle's first response, but soon after, he admitted to his actions. The lead pastor went with her uncle to the local authorities, and he was sentenced to seven years in prison. During that time, Hope's aunt petitioned for a divorce; after she received it, she moved to another village many miles away.

Hope continued to grow, but as she grew, fear grew as well. She began to fully understand what had happened to her. It scared her that most of her innocence had been taken and she didn't even know it.

Her father was hurting too.

He was meant to be the leader and protector of his family, but he could not keep his daughter safe from harm in his own home. Hope did not blame him for what happened, but she knew he blamed himself. Her father's broken heart hurt her even more.

It was difficult to find joy in anything anymore. Even dancing lost its power to take away her pain for just a moment. Lies from the enemy began to take root in her mind, and for a time she believed them. Lies such as, "No man will want you after he finds out you're damaged. You're not beautiful. No one likes you because you're too quiet and insecure. Your family is falling apart because your uncle is in prison."

Depression began to settle in her heart and she could not find a way out. Her parents and sister tried to help her, but they were at a loss as well. They had never seen the darkness of depression like this before. The only thing Hope wanted was for the pain in her heart and soul to stop. She couldn't see the light. But her mother kept encouraging her to put her faith in God.

Even though she couldn't feel or see His light, she couldn't let go of Him.

What would have been the alternative? To let deeper darkness of depression take over? To cut herself in order to release some sort of emotional pain through her physical body? No, she couldn't do that. No matter how many times she contemplated it, she wouldn't let herself go that far. Sometimes, it would take all the strength she had to simply whisper the name of Jesus and that was enough.

Ripples:

1.) Have you ever doubted your self-worth because of something someone said or did to you? Have you ever asked God to reveal your true identity to you?

2.) What does the bible say about healing and pain?

3.) Do you know someone who went through a similar experience? Pray for that person and trust in God to heal her or him.

Write what you feel, hear, or sense from the Holy Spirit

Illustrate any pictures or scenes

He shows you

Jumping Into Revelation

The Journey of Hope: A True Story of Damage, Darkness, and Forgiveness Part Two

By the time Hope was sixteen, her father had lost his position at the local bank and her family had to move to a new village. They didn't realize it at the time, but this move was a blessing from God. They were able to start afresh. Instead of her parents being leaders in the local church, they were able to rest and be supported by the church leadership in their new village.

In this new place, Hope was able to begin her healing process. She joined a group with people her own age who carried a passion for God in a way she had never seen before. Their passion was like a fire in their bones, and she wanted that passion they carried. Little by little her heart started to open, to receive light, to receive joy, to receive hope from the Lord through the people around her. But she still carried the pain of brokenness.

As Hope continued to open her heart to the light of God's truth, she had an opportunity to visit another country and share the love of God with people who were hurting. Even though she was further along in her own healing process, she didn't feel completely whole. She often wondered how God could use her to minister to those who were hurting if she was still in pain. Despite her fears and anxieties, she went on the voyage.

While she was there, she was able to minister to women and young girls who came from similar situations as she did with her uncle. After she shared her faith journey with a few members of her team, her site leader told her, "Because of what you have been through, you can give hope to people. Your life has demonstrated that God can heal them of their brokenness just as He is doing with you." That word of truth remained with Hope for the rest of her life. But her journey was not yet over.

Ripples:

1.) Have you ever felt so broken that you felt like God couldn't use you?

2.) Do you realize that God can use your brokenness to bring restoration and healing to those around you?

3.) What opportunities has God given you to share your journey with someone else?

Write what you feel, hear, or sense from the Holy Spirit

Illustrate any pictures or scenes

He shows you

Jumping Into Revelation

The Journey of Hope: A True Story of Damage, Darkness, and Forgiveness Part Three

After Hope's voyage home, she attended a Bible institute for three years. During her time there, she was able to lay down all of her pain, all of her brokenness, and all of her shame at Jesus' feet. By learning to trust in God more, her relationship with Him was able to grow deep and flourish. Through her growing relationship with the Lord, she was able to dance for Him in worship in a way she had not experienced before. It was beautiful, freeing, and she could feel Him smiling on her as she danced for her audience of One.

However, her growth in freedom could only go so far, for she still carried unforgivingness in her heart toward her uncle. She hadn't seen him since the night the church pastors and her father confronted him, but the memory of him and what he had done was still engraved in her mind. How could she forgive him? What did forgiveness entail? Did she trust God enough to let Him be her vindicator, judge, and loving Heavenly Father? With these thoughts raging in her mind, she began to fall into a depression once again.

In her last year at the Bible institute, she read two books that explained what forgiveness was in a way she could understand. [1] She learned that forgiveness is a choice, not a feeling. It doesn't excuse the action, but it does release the forgiver from any bitterness toward the one who is forgiven. A prime example of what forgiveness looks like is how Jesus freely forgave His enemies as He died on the cross. [2]

In that time of depression, Hope could feel that bitterness was like a weed choking out any life in her that wanted to grow more with God. She could hold onto bitterness and unforgiveness, or she could hold onto God and continue to trust Him. She couldn't hold on to both. The choice was clear.

Yes, it was difficult. Yes, it was painful to acknowledge the hurt. Yes, she had to forgive her uncle again and again when hurtful memories came up, but in that first action of choosing to forgive her uncle, all signs of depression left her and she didn't struggle with the darkness of depression again. By forgiving her uncle, Hope was set free.

The journey of Hope continues, and the light of God's hope will always remain.

Ripples:

1.) Read Romans 8.

2.) Forgiveness. What do you think of when you hear this word?

3.) Have you been able to forgive those that hurt you?

[1] These were two books by Neil T. Anderson. The first was "Victory Over the Darkness" and the second was "The Bondage Breaker".
[2] See Luke 23:34.

Write what you feel, hear, or sense from the Holy Spirit

Illustrate any pictures or scenes

He shows you

Jumping Into Revelation

Trust

So beautiful - and yet so unpredictable.
Untamable - but somehow also tender.
Could it be, that I've been blind
And now I see what's been there all along?

Is it possible – to find that what I'm running from
is truly what I've been longing for
all this time?

And here you are, your arms are wide
I long to come and to confide
In You.

But are you strong enough
to carry all that I have done?
What if this love
can't cover up my hurt and wrong?

And you say

Come closer my love, Come closer my bride
you were meant to be seen, not to cower and hide.
I know it's terrifying, but please be so bold
just follow what's written, not what you've been told.
I'm NOT angry at you, I won't hurt you, my child.
Just take a step forward
I'll be right beside
On the way to the cross
where 2 worlds collide.

Jumping Into Revelation

Could it be that simple?
How could it be true?

If what you say is right,
then what can I do?

Come closer my darling, come closer my heart
We were meant to be 1 not to be far apart.
Can't you see that I love you?
Can't you see that I care?
I hope you come closer
I wish you would dare.
'Cause I paid the cost
There's no debt too steep
I carry the Lost
You're one of my sheep.

I hesitate
What if I go?
What if I say no?
What if I try?
What if I fly?
What if...
You hold out your hand and wait.

Ripple Questions:

1.) Sometimes the hurts inflicted on us from other people can cause us to lose trust in God.

2.) Do you hear His voice calling you to trust in Him despite your hurts?
Would you take His hand?

3.) In what ways will you allow Him to lead you out of darkness and into His victory?

Write what you feel, hear, or sense from the Holy Spirit

Illustrate any pictures or scenes

He shows you

Jumping Into Revelation

Deep Dive: Colossians 2:15

"He disarmed the rulers and authorities and put them to open shame, by triumphing over them in him." - Colossians 2:15 ESV

Finding the true "fullness"

The city of Colossae was a hub of spiritual activity in the ancient world. The Colossians had an array of religious beliefs and views to observe and choose from: Judaism, Christianity, the Greek pantheon of gods, as well as a plethora of mystery religions with their secretive rites and hidden knowledge. Now while the Colossian Christians had walked in the truth for a time, Paul was somewhat concerned that they may have compromised their faith due to the overwhelming influence from the other religions and their adherents. Paul wrote the epistle to the Colossians to further establish them in the faith and to help them to stand strong in it. One of the most powerful sections in this letter is within chapter two.

One of the greatest threats that the early church encountered was the Gnostics. Gnosticism was a mystery religion that combined a number of views. It primarily used a semi-Christian worldview as its base, but then proceeded to commingle it with aspects of Greek mythology, Eastern mysticism, and Judaism. There were a number of Gnostic sects from the second half of the first century going into the second century, and while they all differed to some degree or another for the most part they held to the same core doctrines or beliefs.

To the Gnostics, salvation consisted not in faith but in *"gnosis,"* or knowledge, in particular, a hidden knowledge that only the initiates of the religion would possess. The Gnostics sought to acquire this knowledge for their personal salvation and for enlightenment. With this view came the idea that the godhead consisted not in a single deity, but within a number of divine emanations of the godhead known as Aeons. This conglomeration of divine entities comprised what was known as the *Pleroma,* or the fullness. The Gnostics desired to have a greater understanding of their hidden "knowledge" and to know the wonders of the "fullness."

These doctrines found a way into the Colossian church through those that had infiltrated the Christian community in an attempt to proselytize its members. Throughout Colossians Paul takes shots at the Gnostics. A primary example is in 2:9 where he states, "For in him the whole fullness of deity dwells bodily," with the word for "fullness" being the same word that the Gnostics used for the Aeons.

Paul, in essence, is saying,

"while these doctrines teach you to run after a multitude of false gods to try and find the fullness of

> the godhead, the true fullness dwells in a single individual: Jesus Christ."

Following this verse Paul encourages them by listing all the amazing feats that Christ has accomplished in them, as well as in the universe. They've been filled with the one who has the "fullness." They've been spiritually circumcised and have put away the old nature with its ungodly desires. They've been assimilated into the very death of Christ through baptism and have been raised with Him to new life through His resurrection. They've been forgiven and cleansed from all of their trespasses and sins, with God the Father nailing all offenses and debt to the cross of His beloved Son. Regardless of what Gnosticism could ever offer them, none of it could possibly compare to what God had done in them and through them!

Paul tops off this section with one of the most vivid and impacting verses in the whole Bible. In 2:15 he says,

> "He disarmed the rulers and authorities and put them to open shame, by triumphing over them in him." (ESV)

When we look further into the ancient Greek of this verse we are able to see with crystal clarity the great spectacle of Christ's victory over the demonic.

The word for "disarmed" means to divest or strip another of something that was once theirs.

This divestment can refer to a number of things: power and authority, material belongings, or even a particular attribute of the individual. So, when it comes to what Christ divested the demonic army of, was it:

    a.) Power and authority
    b.) Material belongings, or
    c.) Particular attributes

If you said d.) All the above, then you're right!

    Christ stripped the demonic army of all that they had and left them stark naked and completely bare to their utter shame. The incredible thing is that this event didn't take place in some remote corner of existence! When we look into the meaning of the word "triumphing" we see that this word simply doesn't do the ancient Greek justice. The word means an acclamatory bacchanal victory procession. A what?!?!
    You see, the ancient Greeks worshiped a deity known as Bacchus, a god of wine and mirth. In celebration of Bacchus they would party, celebrate, and parade through the streets in honor of their god. So, when we see this word in Colossians 2:15 it means much more than simply "triumphing." This single verse denotes that when Christ was victorious over the demonic realm through his sacrifice on the cross, He then proceeded to strip the enemy of all that they had and

paraded them through the spiritual realms as an example of His true power and authority. And yet, with this awesome picture there's still one more detail to take note of!

Notice how the verse ends with, "...triumphing over them in him." When you take a step back and observe the context of the proceeding two verses it clearly shows that all that was accomplished through Christ was the work of God the Father! It's as if God the Father was saying through this grand event,

"You see these wretched creatures before you? They mocked me! They scorned me! They rejected my Lordship, but my beloved Son has overcome them! He has triumphed over them and utterly plundered them of all that they had and all that they are! Give glory, and honor, and praise to the Lamb Who sits upon the throne!"

Far too often we give the enemy the glory, and therefore the victory. This should never be the case, brothers and sisters! If Christ has defeated these pathetic rebels and has absolutely laid their kingdom waste, then we need to stand in the faith that lays hold of that victory and rejoice in the fact that we're in Christ! If we're in Christ, that means that His victory is also our victory! He crushed the head of the serpent, and you're a part of His body, that means that Satan is crushed under your feet as well! Walk in this truth and understand the greatness of our God and Savior!!!

Ripples:

1.) How often have you despaired over the power of the enemy in your life and allowed him to shake your faith? Confess these shortcomings to the Lord and know that God is faithful to establish you in Christ. He'll never leave you, nor forsake you!

2.) Think of all of the victories that Christ has granted you in your life. Did you always give Him the glory in these triumphs? Did you give Him thanks and allow His grace to strengthen you in these times of victory? Make it a goal from now on to give Him all the glory in every situation in your life, both the good and the bad.

3.) God is King, Lord, Savior, Father, Comforter, and so much more, and you have access to Him every moment of every day. How do you picture God? Illustrate what you see on the following page.

Write what you feel, hear, or sense from the Holy Spirit

Illustrate any pictures or scenes

He shows you

Jumping Into Revelation

The Love of the King
A Dream

In front of the palace in England, the good king is inside dying. His double is outside about to address a big crowd. I'm close behind the king's adviser who is trying to prepare the king's double for the speech.

The double is very rude and impatient. The speech will have something to do with passing on the kings place to someone new after his death.

All of a sudden the real king who is supposed to be dying in bed quietly walks out of the door behind the double and the whole crowd is amazed!

The first thing the king does is that he notices a large group of children playing on the lawn. A grin lights up his face that seems to light up the whole day. This king who is supposed to be dying takes a great running start down the hill and makes a gigantic belly dive right in the middle of the children. The impact of his chest on the ground would have broken my chest I think. He wrestles, and jokes, and plays roughly and joyfully with the children who recognized him the instant he exited the door. Out of all of his subjects, they missed him most of all. He must have played with them often. In appearance, he greatly resembled Donald Sutherland. He reminded me of how my uncle had treated us when we were children.

When I saw the king's face light up and the love the children and he had for each other, it brought weeping to my eyes; hot tears and even sobbing because of the beauty of the love between them that I was witnessing. It was the most beautiful thing I had ever witnessed.

I woke up weeping because of witnessing such pure love. It was BEAUTIFUL, indescribable the relationship that the king had with those children.

There was a clear distinction between the double and the real king. The double disdained everyone. The king was the opposite. The double was proud. The king was LOVING.

Long live the king!

Ripples:

1.) What differences separate the true from the false?

2.) What similarities are there between the true king and your perspective of God the Father?

3.) What new light has this shed for you on the love of God for His children?

Write what you feel, hear, or sense from the Holy Spirit

Illustrate any pictures or scenes

He shows you

Jumping Into Revelation

The Threshold

We humbly approach Your threshold
Bowing before Your eternal gates
It's Your enduring love we long for
And Your holy presence we await

Open the gates, open the Heavens
Let Your favor rain down on us
Wash us from the places we've been
And bid us to come and to enter in

We stand before You the veil is torn
Open Heavens now touching Earth
The cracking sound of four golden horns
And a thousand angels marching forth

Angel voices in declaration, now with men
Of His power, glory, grace and worth
"Be exalted, O God, above the heavens!
Let Your glory be over all the Earth!"

Ps. 78:23, 136:2
Isa. 45:8, Ps. 24:7
Rev. 9:13, Matt. 27:51
Ps. 57:5

Jumping Into Revelation

Ripple, Ripple, Ripple:

Let the presence of the Holy Spirit ripple through you as a stone of revelation drops into a quiet pond. Let His everlasting ripples expand as they spread from you to others in ever-expanding rings that change every place they touch. You are a ripple of the Spirit. You are sent out into the people as a fresh move of the Spirit. As you go, take His presence with you and be the change their souls cry out for.

Write what you feel, hear, or sense from the Holy Spirit

Illustrate any pictures or scenes
He shows you

Jumping Into Revelation

Appendix

Prophetic Dream Interpretation

Dreams have gotten much criticism from the church over the years, but things are changing. The church is becoming increasingly more accepting of dreams as a way the Lord speaks today. Since there is still some skepticism and extra caution around the areas of dreams and their interpretations, I thought that I would answer a few common questions to ease any possible concerns.

Are dreams for today?

Many Christians have been taught that dreams were for the prophets in the Old Testament and already served their purpose. They claim that when Jesus, the Word, came there was no longer any need for dreams so they are not for today. Therefore, dreams most likely come from the enemy for the purpose of raising up false prophets. In a sense, dreamers today are likely false prophets so guard yourself from them. One common verse used to support this idea is Hebrews 1:1-2, stating, "God spoke to our fathers by the prophets but in these last days He has spoken to us by His Son." The truth of this matter lies in the

Word of God as well as the nature of God. He reveals Himself to the world so that they are without excuse on the day of judgment (Romans 1:18-20.) He did not stop using prophets to reveal Himself, nor did He limit the amount of ways in which He reveals Himself. He, in fact, increased His revelation through Jesus by giving dreams and visions to everyone. God becoming human, with His death and resurrection, He tore the veil, allowing humans to identify with God through His ministry. Now we can go directly to God instead of a prophet. The ministry of a prophet was no longer restricted to a few prophets in the land, but opened up to every human to receive the same revelation. This means that God poured His Spirit out on all flesh so that all, even unbelievers, can receive dreams and visions from the Lord (Acts 2:17-18). Everyone has the ability of an Old Testament prophet. Peter's purpose for mentioning Joel's prophecy was to point out that those days are now here: we are in these last days. God is increasing revelation of Himself, not decreasing it.

Are dreams from God or from Satan?

The Word of God reveals to us that many dreams come from God. The opening line of a passage often opens with a variant of "Then, God said to him in a dream." You can find this in Genesis 20:3, 6, 31:11, 24, 40:8, 41:25 and 1 Kings 3:5.

Dreams from the enemy are also possible. Eliphaz, Job's companion, admitted to having a vision of an evil spirit at night with a deceitful message (4:11-21).

It is possible to have dreams from God or evil spirits, so it is important to learn how to distinguish the difference according to the Word of God. In a word of encouragement, I would like to add that it is not difficult to tell the difference. Please don't allow fear of mistaking evil for the Lord prevent you from hearing what the Lord has to say. The best way to discern the source of a dream is to interpret its meaning. Daniel said, in Daniel 5:11, that all interpretations belong to the Lord. When we discern His voice in a dream He gives it reveals His heart, His personality, His love, and His will for your life. When you interpret a dream from the enemy it reveals their lies, hatred, and schemes.

Interpretations are the key to discerning the source of a dream or vision.

How can you know the difference?

There are many descriptions in the Bible regarding the mannerisms of the Lord versus evil spirits. One of the most descriptive passages is found in James 1:13-17, Let no one say when he is tempted, "I am being tempted by God," for God cannot be tempted with evil, and he himself tempts no one. [14] But each person is tempted when he is lured and enticed by his own desire. [15] Then desire when it has conceived gives birth to sin, and sin when it is fully grown brings forth death." So that nobody can say that God is tempting one to sin and so the enemy cannot cause confusion by trying to impersonate Him, He has expressed how He speaks to us, this includes dreams. If you felt tempted in anyway in the dream, it is not from God. If you felt lured or enticed by your own desire in the dream it is not from God. Dreams from the enemy lead to sin and death. Dreams from the Father lead to what is good and perfect. He is the Father of Lights and only sends

Lights; benevolent spirits, not dark ones. There is no variation of color or lights in shadows or darkened hues. If you dream in bright, vibrant colors, it is from the Lord, if you dream in dark hues or shadows, it is from the enemy. The Lord gives us very clear instruction to discern His voice because He doesn't want us to miss what He is telling us.

How do I know these dreams are from God?

This question becomes a little more personal because it requires a certain level of interpretation. This should not be an alarming statement, because we must handle the Bible in the same fashion. When the Spirit gives us a verse to chew on it has a proper interpretation in its context and a personal application for us at the moment. It is inappropriate to pull statements from the Bible out of context to interpret according to our will. This is also true of dream interpretation. We must carefully discern what the Lord is saying in either revelation and weigh its meaning against the Word of God for accuracy and application. When discerning dreams and their interpretations we ought to follow Paul's advice in 1 Thess. 5:19-21, "Do not quench the Spirit. Do not despise prophecies, but test everything; hold fast to what is good." Following this advice will begin to strengthen your level of discerning His voice in dreams so that you will know which are from the Lord and which are not.

How seriously should I take these dreams?

I try to take my dreams as seriously as Joseph, Daniel, and Solomon did. The dreams that Joseph had were a revelation of his identity and the purpose the Lord set out for him. The dreams the Lord gave him became true and saved Israel from a deadly famine that would have wiped out their nation. Joseph didn't know the plans of the Lord and neither do I. I trust Him to do what He does and cooperate with Him when He lets me in on what He wants to do in my life.

Daniel received a dream from the Lord about the future and the first thing he did when he awoke was to write it down so that he could share it with others. The dreams the Lord gives to us are not always just for ourselves, but sometimes they are for others that cannot yet perceive what the Lord wants them to know. If I am the person He chooses to minister on His behalf to others, I take this responsibility seriously.

It was in a dream that God imparted wisdom to Solomon and if there is an impartation of the Spirit in dreams given to me, I want to receive that impartation (1 Kings 3:5).

Dreams have become a way that I listen to the Lord and a way that I receive what He gives me on a daily, or nightly, basis. He tells me about myself from His perspective, He gives me guidance, He answers my questions, He gives me grace, peace, and deliverance in my dreams. He teaches me about the world around me and reveals what is taking place in the spiritual realm that I don't see with my physical eyes. My dreams are a blessing that draws me close to my Father's side where I can follow Him wherever He goes. I take our nightly conversations more seriously than I can accurately communicate to you.

What are you asking me to do with the dreams in this devotional?

This is a funny question, because I'm really not asking for much from you. The dreams we share in this devotional are more of an invitation into a way that the Spirit reveals Himself. I simply want to invite you into this particular way in which the Holy Spirit reveals Himself. Perhaps it's new to you, or strange, or even concerning. There was a time that it was new to me as well, and concerning as I sought to understand thoughts that are higher than my thoughts. I don't want to miss a thing He says, you know? As far as being strange or weird, my dreams are very strange and weird, but the metaphors are rich, the meanings are multi- layered, and the revelations are deep. We are listening to an all-powerful, all-knowing, eternal being, Who is the source of all wisdom. Things that seem strange or weird are a revealed limitation of my own understanding, but that's okay, I'm only but a child. I have an eternity to discover Him and I have just begun. I extend an invitation to you to come with us. Let's jump into this revelation together and see what the Spirit has to say to you. So, as the gift He has given me to perceive Him, I impart it to you. I bless you with dreams and visions of the Heavenly Father and with visitations of Jesus in your dreams. All that I ask is that when you lay down to rest, that you receive what He desires to show you. May you continuously draw closer and closer to the Father's side, through the precious name of Jesus.

-Andrew Fulton

Kingdom Profiles

Aaron Longacre

Aaron Longacre has a great desire to obey the voice of the Lord. He strikes an amazing balance between prophet and teacher that yields tremendous spiritual fruit. With a deep love for God's word and a heart that seeks after the truth, his desire to make truth easier for others to reach is evident through his writing. He has a tremendous ability to bring the best of the Spirit in our written works and helps clear away any soulish thoughts to allow the Spirit to clearly shine through.

Andrew Fulton

Andrew Fulton has a heart for individuals to come into their full authority in Christ and to know who they are in Him. As an equipper of the saints, and a prophetic writer and dreamer, his gift as an in-depth teacher of the word always seeks to instill a passion in his listeners for the Father's heart. He knows who he is in the kingdom and has no fear in walking in his God-given destiny as a natural leader in the body of Christ.

Allison Lozo

Allison Lozo has a tremendous sensitivity to words and pictures by the Holy Spirit. She seems to be in the Spirit every time we see her and is constantly chasing and in lock step with the Spirit. She is a shining example of a Proverbs 31 woman with great character, strength, spiritual discernment, and wisdom beyond her physical years. Her tender heart of compassion for the hurting reaches out as a voice of encouragement to the victim with a ministry of empowerment in the Holy Spirit.

Aaron Loyet

Aaron Loyet is steady, constant, loyal, and has a heart for missions. His caring and sensitive heart aids his gift of mercy for the lost and those that are poor in spirit. As a man of few words in a crowd, when he does speak, we listen carefully as he dispenses great wisdom and insight. He is also an excellent photographer.

Mark Marini

Mark Marini is an out of the box thinker with the calling of a change agent. The Spirit of God sends Mark to those that need or desire change, but lack the necessary personnel or encouragement to do it. He carries the spirit of joy that is tangible when he walks into a room. He is also an amazing prophetic musician that ushers in the presence of the Holy Spirit.

Benjamin Mummau

Benjamin Mummau is an overcomer, a warrior that wins the fight, and one who goes back into battle to fight for others. He has no concern for popularity and has no fear of man. Though his topics of writing are weighty, he is full of joy, kind-hearted, courageous, and fun to be around. His calling is to expose the desires of the flesh for what they are, in order to set God's people free.

Sarah Koch

Sarah Koch is a sweet-spirited seer/writer with an amazing gift for writing poetry. She often expresses a deep love for the written Word of God and the truths that lay within. She has an eye for beauty, and expresses the loving relationship of the Father for His children in great detail.

Jumping Into Revelation

A Special Word of Thanks

We would like to give a special thanks to the generous donors who made this publication possible.
Thank you for your love and support.
We couldn't have done this without you! May God bless you as this devotional blesses those who read it and experience the presence of the Lord.

Threshold Church
The Longacre Family
Dale and Barbara Works
Ralph Mounts
The Doner Family
Pamela Henry
Mary and Will Baldree
Mariam Sarkessian
Kit and Terri Fulton
Paul Broomell

Upcoming titles
from the authors of

Overcoming Waters Publications

Jumping Into Revelation: The Heavenly Realms
The V.I.P. Revelation
The Journey of Hope
24 Levels of Revelation
Open My Eyes Dream Ministry Series
The Haunted House That Needed Help
The Sword and the Trowel
Letters From a Daughter's Desk
The Wilderness and the Cave

If you enjoyed this devotional please leave a good review and a comment on our

Amazon Page and
Facebook Page

Made in the USA
Middletown, DE
15 February 2019